For the high and mighty

Also by Sophia Hembeck

Things I Have Noticed – Essays on leaving/searching/finding

Muse Letter Publishing
Edinburgh, 2023

Things I Have Loved – A collection (sort of) by Sophia Hembeck
Artwork by Sophia Hembeck

ISBN 978-1-3999-4580-6

Typeset in Baskerville

Sophia Hembeck

Things I Have Loved

– A collection (sort of)

first edition
published 2023, Edinburgh
– 1st print 2023 –

I ~~don't~~ care about ~~you and your fucking~~ feelings.

Is what you said to me and I never answered you then.
I just let it sink in.

It took me minutes, and hours, and months.
I counted them all. Every inch of time passing by.

And now that it has, I can just say:

Well, I do.

CONTENT

Perhaps This Is Where Childhood Ends | 1

FLOWERS.

Perhaps This Is Where Childhood Ends | 2

SUMMER.

Perhaps This Is Where Childhood Ends | 3

COLD WATER.

Perhaps This Is Where Childhood Ends | 4

OYSTERS.

Parachutes Couldn't Carry Us Higher | 1

DANCE.

Parachutes Couldn't Carry Us Higher | 2

KISSING GIRLS.

Parachutes Couldn't Carry Us Higher | 3

The Lost Empress | 1

BOOKS.

The Lost Empress | 2

VIENNA.

The Lost Empress | 3

PARIS.

The Lost Empress | 4

fuck this then.

Acknowledgements

If you think of childhood as its own world, a magical realm of imagination, a world that is partly made up by whatever coping mechanisms your child-brain fabricates to keep you safe and whole.

Where there's always a happy ending, a twist, a spell to change life's course.

—*Then this is where it ended.*

Perhaps This Is Where Childhood Ends

1

"Why don't you love me?"

I'm ten and crying. Next to me the discus fish are floating up and down, the fish my father loves so much are swimming in circles. The Wells is cleaning the aquarium as he always does. He is huge and one usually feels very tempted to knock on the glass to force a reaction. In a few years the Wells will die and my dad will dry and prop him up and store him in a cupboard in the basement. Eventually he will become too fragile to clean and will gather dust.

Just like this memory.

If the fish knew what monumental scene was about to take place they might stop and pay attention. Alas, they are fish and unaware of any drama. Everything they see is warped and distorted through the thick aquarium glass.

Like all memories.

I have played it over and over in my head ever since I might as well have invented it, as it has all the qualities of a dream: I have no sense of what was before, no reason of why I was there, where it started, why it happened, it is a completely isolated loop in the time and space continuum of my mind where all my self-worth seems to get stuck.

"Why don't you care about me?"

No answer.

We will come back to that.

FLOWERS.

They were never good at buying flowers anyway. None of them.

Mrs. Dalloway said she would buy the flowers herself.[1]

I rip out some sweet peas, cornflowers, and white cosmos, they're dangling in my hand as I wait for the Uber to arrive to take my stuff to another place.

I look at the garden that is bursting and overflowing onto the path. 3 months ago I had shovelled, torn, broken up the soil, I had sown seeds and watered and waited impatiently and now it is all there in all its glory: the harvest of a dream and time for me to wake up.

There's a Welsh word that I came across a couple of days ago: *hiraeth*. It describes a feeling of longing for something that is irretrievably lost – "a unique blend of place, time and people that can never be recreated. This unreachable nature adds an element of grief, but somehow it is not entirely unwelcome."[2]

It's similar to the German word *Sehnsucht* or the Portuguese *saudade*. A homesickness for something that in a real way may have never even been like that, a reconciliation with pain.

One eye laughing, one eye crying as you leave. A soothing Bittersweet.

– That is where I live right now.

---

[1] Virginia Woolf, Mrs. Dalloway, Hogarth Press 1925

[2] https://www.bbc.com/travel/article/20210214-the-welsh-word-you-cant-translate

Things I Have Loved

When I look at the flowers on my desk, I see it all, that there was love, dedication, hope.

Once.

And what was *not* there.

What *is*.

People wonder after a break-up, after a loss: Where does the love go? Is it blown away like dandelion puffs? To be sown in better places? Or can I take that love – take it all – and let the seeds fall onto me?

This time.

A wildflower meadow waiting to bloom.

Perhaps This Is Where Childhood Ends

2

There's a train station in my hometown that is haunted by a ghost. To be precise, there are four stations, but only one that gives me shivers every time I pass by. I rarely stop there, there's nothing for me to do in that area but remember.

And remember me remembering and multiplying ghosts till the whole station is filled with them. Overflowing onto the rails, hiding in the bushes, under benches.

I try not to look out of the window when that happens. When everything is covered in white mist, I could get snow-blind.

I always slept with my door open when I was a child. Leaving the door open had always felt safe; my parents sitting downstairs in the living room watching TV, my three siblings walking up and down the stairs to go to the bathroom, the light in the hall that would shine for half a minute then go off by itself. Somehow the open door meant that we were all connected, somehow sleeping amongst each other. Closing the door would have meant I was alone, unprotected, cast outside the family realm.

Shortly after turning thirteen, however, I shut the door, coinciding with the time I phoned a boy from school that I had gone out with four or five times to tell him: *that it was over*.

I remember sitting on the toilet in my family home, the boy still sitting on my bed waiting for me to come back, looking at the tiny bright red circles on the toilet paper. He had scratched my labia while trying to get his fingers inside. He had been the first boy to ever get near and I had an inkling this would only get worse. I sat there on the cold toilet seat, the skylight above me blowing a sharp spring wind into my neck, afraid to go back, afraid to face him and tell him that I wanted him to leave. My room, my house suddenly a war zone and me hiding in the trenches. I had said no in the end, hadn't I? *Could he not see how uncomfortable he was making me?*

It felt surreal, the blood and the pain, as if it was happening to someone else. I remember the disappointment, the sadness, the numbness; I don't remember being angry at him. I only remember thinking how my words had not exactly landed. And how conflicted that had made me feel.

Had I not used the right words?

My sister said to me this year during Christmas holidays how I often was unaware of the things that were happening around me. In that case she meant: how I had not reacted to something she wanted to show me.

But I wonder how often in life I had been unaware when people were actually hurting me?

–

Eventually he left. I don't remember what I said to him, if I actually told him off or if I just politely came up with an excuse. If I went down to my parents and pretended he didn't exist. It's all a haze now. Some parts vivid as if I was still there, my hand pressing against his forearm, the colour of my underwear: pink. Other parts blurry: did he feel sorry? Did he understand the situation? Did he care?

All I know is that I waited for the Easter holidays to arrive that were due a couple of days later. That I made the plan to call him and to end it in the safety of two free weeks without having to see him at school.

My door stayed shut after that day.

–

"Did something happen to you?" My mum asked me a while after Easter, looking at a pretty dark painting I was drawing but I shrugged it off and assured her that I was okay, that I was just painting *whatever*. I don't think I had the words then. The words had failed me. They were not safe to land anywhere. So why bother? Rebecca Solnit writes about this silencing, that actually isn't a silencing at all, as that would presume "someone attempted to speak. In my case, it wasn't silencing because no speech was stopped; it never started, or it had been stopped so far back I don't remember how it happened. It never occurred to me to speak to the men who pressured me then, because it didn't occur to me that I had the authority to assert myself thus or that they had any obligation or inclination to respect my assertions, or that my words do anything but make things worse."[3]

–

13 years later I would lie in a bed, my bed, in a city that I would leave again eventually, and I would lie there with the same feeling. That somehow my words had not landed again, that they had slipped off this person, this person that I had slept with a couple of times before but that was now supposed to be my friend and who for some reason felt so invited to walk over my boundaries that I eventually gave in and had the worst sex of my life. Where boundaries are being pulled and pushed and pre-conceptions work like mechanisms, to entrap.

And I want to ask, where is this coming from? This compliance.

---

[3] Rebecca Solnit, Recollections of My Non–Existence, Viking 2020

And I want to ask: did you care? Did you notice?

Because all I know is that: my words had not landed and when they don't, there are only two things in those moments that you can choose: you play along and pretend you never meant them. You invalidate yourself. Or you stay firm and possibly face repercussions that you have no control over.

It feels like summoning ghosts.

There's a train station in my hometown that is haunted by a ghost. To be precise, there are four stations, but only one that gives me shivers every time I pass by. I rarely stop there, there's nothing for me to do in that area but remember.

And remember me remembering and multiplying ghosts till the whole station is filled with them. Overflowing on to the rails, hiding in the bushes, under benches.

I try not to look out of the window when that happens. When everything is covered in a white mist, I could get snow-blind.

I write those words years later in my yet to be finished novel, finally finding the words. The only way to get rid of a ghost is to stare it in the face and say its name. In fairy tales, potent enemies lose their power once you call them by their true name, like *Rumpelstilzchen*.

My magic consists of crafting stories, binding words into spells and capturing my foes between the soft binding of two sheets of paper.

But to get to that point, you have to acknowledge the ghosts.

You have to see them first.

And how many.

SUMMER.

We make plans, we book flights, book hotels and airbnb's, we look up restaurants and places to see/to go/to love/to hate/to be excited/to rest and relax. We look at the weather report, we dream up the time away.

And then and then and then–

It's early June or late July or mid-August and the summer has laid out its cards, there on the table, up for grabs: the memories we wanted to make and didn't get.

A summer rarely behaves. This summer is not behaving at all. It's raised two middle fingers in the air, blocking the view.

One morning at 4am, still awake from worry, I walk to the beach, the sky blue and bright, the sun taking its time to rise over the horizon. I have yet to know what I know now: whatever happens in the next days, weeks, months. *This will always be here for you.*

And I walk home to what is still my home and two mornings later I walk out, forever.

This summer is not behaving at all. It's cold and wet and I wear turtlenecks and get anxious about the climate. I'm heartbroken and the rain fits. At least that. At least something does.

Madonna is singing repeatedly about the power of goodbye. Nobody is asking me what I'm going to do this summer, they all sigh and hug and offer spare rooms. No more rapid changes, I ought to stay still. But the Uber driver thinks I'm beautiful. And Ryanair is not refunding anything.

The music in my ears is very very loud when I walk through the city at night. Drunk on too much red wine. I imagine myself as a dancing hot mess. Walking through Cowgate, I pass by the joyful masses, the blissful summer revellers and continue towards the unknown.

This summer is not behaving and I am intending to do the same.

Most days I wake up at 5am now. There's no point, no reason why I should start the morning so early but my body seems to think otherwise so I let it be. I lie and I dream of a future that feels just within my reach. I've always done that. Live more in the future than the present, in the better world, looking for the better me.

I eat apples, two a day. And I think of this passage by Louise Erdrich from *The Painted Drum* where she writes about how life will break you and that after all there is no protection or solution to prevent this. That this is a truth of life, even still sitting under an apple tree and watching the apples fall, their sweetness wasted, one should try to taste as many as possible.

And I do. I do everything now. I don't care anymore that I care so much. I start curating a dating profile; I cry on my way through the meadows; I meet my friends and talk for hours as they patiently wait for me to get better; I walk through the city smiling and lifting my hands high above me feeling a sense of relief. Something that was dormant awakens. I write angry notes that I never send, I go to an event alone, I let the bouncer at the door hit on me. He tells me how he once rescued a woman from drowning and he asks: that water looks quite sparkly? And I say: that's because there's gin in it. He doesn't tell me that I am not allowed to drink alcohol outside the venue but he barks at everyone else to keep their drinks inside. *This is how I know.* – And then I leave in the middle because I get sad again. Because I can't bear to be alone in that moment. Because I am doing everything but not all at once and putting myself first, from now on.

I watch *Downton Abbey* and I feel solace in the way everyone is repressing their feelings as if that was possible and when I press play the first thing one of the ladies says is:

"Aren't all of us stuck with the choices we make?"

And I laugh because it's true. Because I guess some apples are bad apples.

But how could you know?

Perhaps This Is Where Childhood Ends

3

There's a video of me on Christmas Eve ca. 1996 where I barge into the house after church proclaiming to the camera:
I'm the star of this family!

I have not seen it since, I am not sure if it even still exists somewhere on a cassette or burned CD, but what I do know is that it exists in the shared memory of my family, because it was frequently pulled out in the following years of my upbringing. There is something about that memory that still strikes me: how my family sees me and how the outside world sees me.

I had always been an imaginative child: I was an amazon, a witch, a mermaid, a warrior princess. A wild girl battling trees with swords she made herself out of thick branches, climbing to the top of the tree crown to enjoy the view. I was smart and asked a lot of questions, I never waited to get permission to do something, which occasionally would lead to almost falling out of a window, a hole in the head, creating toxic fumes in the cellar; I would routinely re-arrange the furniture in my room when I felt I needed a change and I would invent stories to shock, such as telling the neighbour's daughter that my brother would be sent to a youth correctional facility. It didn't feel like lying. I liked to try things on to see if they fit, what they would feel like. One of my friend's brothers was actually sent away and I guess it sounded interesting. So when I barged into the family home, declaring *I am a star*, it was a role I wanted to try on.

I remember both scenes. The actual one where I thought it would be funny to say something like that to the camera, to somehow let future me and potentially *the world* know whom they would have to reckon with. I imagined it quite hilarious if in later years I, in fact, would turn out to be *a star,* and wouldn't that be marvellous to see me announce it already at such a young age? I also remember the other version. The perspective from the viewer, seeing a tall blond girl with a boyish haircut over-excitedly (yet not without charm) take centre stage in the family album.

And then there is another scene, one that is hidden underneath all of that: a stream of emotions washing over me as I continuously learned to behave otherwise.

How I have never entered a room like that again.

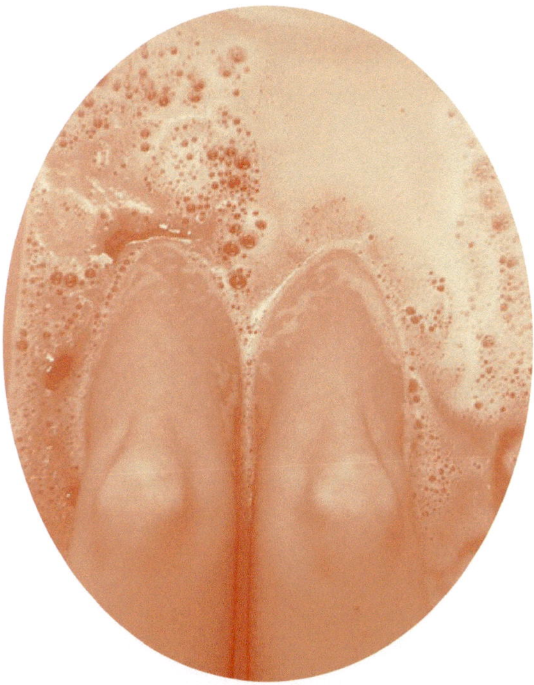

COLD WATER.

"If you take care of the small things, the big things take care of themselves. You can gain more control over your life by paying closer attention to the little things." Emily Dickinson once said.

It's been 12 days since I started to wake up in the morning, study the tide chart and decide when to walk to the beach, and immerse myself in the cold, very cold waters of Portobello bay.

12 days of just doing it, without huge effort, just trusting that it will somehow help, not questioning it. It's easy: the beach is 3 minutes away, I just go in my bathing suit, in and out, done.

I still cry every day. Unfortunately one cannot freeze emotions.

But I don't question that either. I let it be, let the emotion like waves wash over, let them startle me from time to time, feel them rising up, especially when I catch myself thinking: I'm definitely done with the crying.

– I am so not.

Unfortunately, there is no tide chart for a broken heart. No estimation, but some clues, hopes, wishes.

I want to believe that it will heal itself if I let it. If I create the space, if I take care of the little things, like showing up for myself, not reacting to every stimulus but pausing, and in doing so, creating options.

Because I do. You do. We all have options all the time but we're so stuck in habitual behaviour that we miss out on them. Only afterwards there is a hint, a glimmer, that things could have been done differently. If we had only waited a second and listened to ourselves.

"You can't read the label when you're in the jar," a friend of mine said to me a couple of weeks ago. Well, the jar is broken now. So fuck the jar anyway.

I guess what I'm trying to say is that: leave the big picture for a moment. Concentrate on yourself. How are you sitting? Is your breathing shallow? Are you clenching your jaw? Are you tired? Hungry? Bored? Inspired? What do you really want to do right now?

Stop thinking of the endgame, the goal. Do you notice the little things that need your attention? The little stepping stones that will take you across the ocean?

Perhaps This Is Where Childhood Ends

4

Somehow everyone has gotten tinier and tinier since I arrived. I'm surrounded by an ever shrinking world. My parents are barely reaching my waist these days. Their voices seem higher than they used to be, ringing in my ears about the next steps that I ought to take, the future I have yet to plan. When I answer they seem terrified, shrinking even more. I'm barely able to see them now.

So far I have broken: the chair I sat on at breakfast, the pen I use to write in my diary, the remote control for the TV. I try to touch things lightly but it's hard when everything is small and fragile around you. It's so easy to misstep, shattering china like a bull.

On my walk this morning I saw a man wearing a blue cap, carrying his baby, seeming to be on the verge of a mental breakdown. Picking his steps as if he'd risk tripping any minute now.

Any minute now.

You know something is wrong when you're standing half-dressed in front of your wardrobe. Wailing into the open doors, grabbing them tightly, as if waiting to be hugged.

When I was little we used to enter the wardrobe and pretend it was a lift to the *Blocksberg*, the place where the witches meet in Germany at *Walpurgisnacht* for the sabbath. One after another we would step in while outside the others would pound their hands against the wood, swooshing and howling to mimic the flight.

There's something so calming about finding yourself in confinement, a defined space where you're protected, even when outside the world is swirling and taking you places.

Pressing my face into the pillow, submerging myself into the soft texture: I have been sleeping a lot lately. In fact, I have been sleeping so much that I am not sure what being awake feels like anymore. There is no contrast to my rest, it is so consuming it's exhausting.

"Quite magical how hydrangeas can change their colour depending on the soil they're growing in." My Mum says while she places the stems in tiny jugs. "It's not up to them though. They *must* change."

In the evening we watch a documentary about the golden twenties in Germany and how Bauhaus – a triste, minimal and function-following design philosophy – was invented, proclaiming a new era of thinking: *beauty is about practicality*. Form follows function. Everyone gets their own bathroom. Hygiene is front and centre.

The first night in my childhood bedroom I listen for noises, particular ones: scratching, shuffling. *Nothing*. Since moving to Edinburgh, my sleep has been interrupted by mice racing through my room. No matter where I move, they are already there.

One night I heard a shuffling behind my pillow. Slowly I rose, turned on the light, my dog Filou lifting his head sleepily, completely useless if not just as terrified; I grabbed the pillow and under it, found a tiny mouse looking at me in disbelief then running off, me screaming: I have never slept the same since.

On my walk the next morning across town I see the result of *Bauhaus* all around me. And I wonder: if your *dream* is a two-bedroom flat with a separate washroom and toilet, are you even dreaming at all?

I try to walk a different path every day. Triggering memories from all over my childhood. I read the names on doorbells, checking if they still live there, realising I don't actually recall their last names. *Is Saskia home? Is Rosalia home?* That's all you needed to say as a child and a door would open and you'd wait in the hallway till they came out to play.

A muscular guy passes by and politely says *Hello* and I try to find something familiar in his face, but I see nothing.

Most of us have left.

—

I sit on a bench with my dad at a birthday party for their neighbour and he asks me how the book is going. This book. The one I am writing right now. I tell him about my fears, my worries. How I want this to be about my childhood and the journey towards self-worth. That it's hard to tell where I am at. I tell him that I have 10,000 good words but I am actually not sure. That I've written some parts that might go into the next one, how it's going to be a trilogy in the end. That I want to write about money and how it affects us. That I think the UK has a charity mindset instead of a solidarity one. That charity is about thinking you have more and so you ought to give in order to be a good person, a better person. And that solidarity is about thinking we're meant to share anyway, we're all the same, because we're all good. *That there is a distinction in hierarchy in this.*

The charity mindset means: I am better (off) than you so I give you charity, you are depending on me. A solidarity mindset is about: I am the same as you so I share my wealth and support you, we are interdependent.

In relationship terms, one would be the toxic behaviour of a partner that wants you to move in with them as a lodger so you essentially have no rights or demands on the space; the other would be the healthier behaviou; a partner who puts you on the mortgage so you both share responsibility and subsequently wealth.

And just like charity the former can sometimes seem more appealing as you don't have to do anything but accept the offer and be grateful.

I take another sip from my *Glühwein.*

But all of this, I tell him, is only an idea for now. That I will need to prove it, that as of now it is a too-vulnerable theory and that I would need more time and data to back this up.

My dad listens patiently to all this and says in the end: *well, I hope it all goes really well for you.* And he means it.

And something happens here. But you can't see it yet.
The ghost that just passed by.

We both look up at the people standing around us, in little groups, some neighbours, some friends, mostly all about 30 years older than me, having lived twice the life I have so far as I realise that I need to re-write this book.

My story, really.

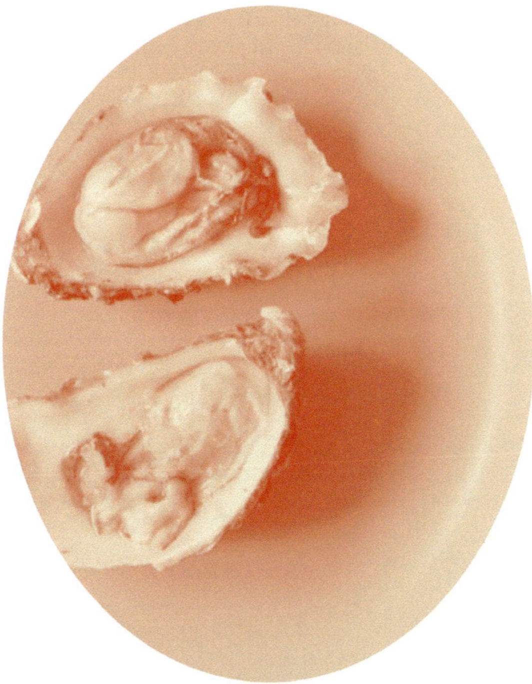

OYSTERS.

"It looks like an eye, that's why I chose it." – "I guess you see things that others don't. Not necessarily looking at the world. But in people. You see them deeply."

I'm sitting at a table made out of oyster shells, around us a translucent curtain suggesting privacy though we are absolutely visible, to anyone passing by. Her fingers are delicate, holding the shell that I chose in her palm, softly tracing the back, pointing out the two spines of this particularly *unusual* oyster, opening the shell softly with expertise. I try not to hold my breath but I probably do, in situations like this, I always hold it in, something about talking to a stranger, in a strange setting, but these are strange times. "So shall we see what the oyster reveals inside? The future it withholds?" I nod.

"What is an oyster reading?" I had asked my friend a couple of weeks before when she mentioned it in a conversation. "I don't know, I guess like a palm reading. It's an art performance," she shrugged her shoulders, "but fun."

And because I like art and fun and knowing about the future, I am sitting here now. Holding my breath. Waiting for this woman, who I find out later is an actress and not necessarily a medium and/or clairvoyant to tell me what is going to happen.

"Oysters have populated the waters of Scotland for millennia, nourishing people living on its coasts. Like a modern palimpsest, oysters record time and events. Similar to tree rings, every season an oyster grows a shell around their lip. As the shell grows it encases the environmental conditions in which they live." So says the event page by the artist collective, *Cooking Sections*, who in their artwork regularly examine "the systems that organise the world through food." I guess this is what I expected, a person reciting a script, telling me about the past/present/future of the oyster, the ecological function it has within the oceanic ecosystem, and the effect the climate crisis has on them.

But this is not really what is happening that Saturday afternoon when I find myself sitting in front of a dozen oysters trying to choose one that speaks to me, *to hear its call.*

"You carry the waters of Scotland inside of you. There's a reason you came here," she says, looking at the shell filled with saltwater. "You open up easily and you bond deeply. When you connect with someone you pour something of yourself into the other person and vice versa. This can sometimes create a shadow inside of you." I'm struck by her words, fighting tears she cannot possibly understand. Is this still art or is this something else? I am wondering and trying to find out whether she actually means it. There is something about a stranger reading you. The things they notice that you cannot see.

And when I ask her afterward how she came to do this job she said: "I wouldn't tell you anything that I don't believe is true. There's no real script. Of course, they give us information about the oysters, how they develop, signs to look out for but– it's an interesting job. I'm not genuinely acting, I'm trying to read you as I speak."

As I walk out of the room, and emotions wash over me like the tide rising, it doesn't really matter to me whether it is true or not, whether the oyster resembles my life or not, it is about the things she said to me, human to human, that I know are true.

Just like this oyster, you have the ability to change.
To grow stronger. Each year.

I talk a lot about you in therapy because I am trying to understand what happened. The carpet is looking weird each time, reminding me of our own when I was little. It has similar colours. The whole office reminds me of my childhood. The curse of Ikea furniture.

Parachutes Couldn't Carry Us Higher

1

There are only a few people in my life so far I have connected with in a way that feels like an unbreakable bond: seeing someone truly and loving them for that. The interesting part is you do not know that when you meet them and at the same time you absolutely do. Or, you hope.

The first time I met Svenja was at a party just after I came back from Thailand; estranged from my old friend circle and unsure where I belonged. We bonded over the fact that neither of us did.

Back then, Svenja would travel through Germany on the weekends to go to concerts and photograph the bands and in a way I thought she was living an *Almost Famous* sort of life. We once interviewed the Swedish band *Sugar Plum Fairy* as I was aspiring to be a journalist at that time. A forgettable indie rock band who were mostly known because they were related to the then very famous band *Mando Diao.* I think, including us, there were five people in the audience. Sitting in a sad, unusually large, green room backstage, Svenja circling me and the band with her camera, it had the ambience of a thirteen year olds birthday party where half of the people didn't show up because there was a better party thrown by one of the popular girls down the street.

Either way, at seventeen Svenja had the *chutzpah* to call the venue and write emails to managers and I think in many ways our friendship was based on the mutual admiration and coolness we subscribed to the other person.

Initially we wanted to move to Berlin after graduating but neither of us got accepted there. So we made do with Bochum.

It all began on a loud street, 10 minutes away from the Bochumer central station in a flat on the second floor with high ceilings and long windows, a little balcony and a two coloured wooden floor. We called our flat *Bananafishboat* after a short story by J.D. Salinger which I just recently have actually read. The story is about a young veteran, traumatised by war, who shoots himself in the head at the end. It is quite a depressing story and I have no recollection as to why we chose to give our flat that name, I guess it sounded cool.

And that was our plan at the beginning of our new lives as university students anyway: to appear as cool as possible.

Looking back we were just young, so very young, we were trying to become by imitation, by surrounding ourselves with the right objects, the right artefacts, signifiers of belonging to create a future where we would have become these versions, our true selves.

I would make new friends, some for a semester, some for life. A time of midnight cheese pasta and singing along to Robbie Williams at the top of our lungs, smoking and talking and laughing at 4am in the morning. Flashing our tits to each other on bridges and some of us nicking fancy glasses at bars and once a whole table that was innocently standing around, heaving it onto a train and then leaving it to its own devices. When the DJs would always play *Where is my mind?* at the end and I always hoped to find some eyes across the room.

Years later I would learn to play that song in a version by Maxence Cyrin to impress a man that didn't care for me, but worse, didn't care for himself at all.

There's a scene Patti Smith describes in her memoir *Just Kids*, I often think of in this regard where she and her lifelong friend Robert Mapplethorpe walk along the promenade, all dressed up and an older couple stopping by, openly observing them, curiously discussing whether they look like artists and the man replying nonchalantly stating in the end: Oh they're just kids.

One could say we were quite pretentious and that would be accurate. We used pages from an Emily Dickinson's poetry collection as wallpaper in our entrance hall. The whole first semester I wore a tiny scarf around my head in an attempt to personify a certain hippiesque chic that was sort of *in* at that time. I would blow soap bubbles during the University strikes wearing a fake sheer coat emulating a modern Gloria Steinem except that back then I didn't even know who Gloria Steinem was.

All I knew was that the air felt electric that time we were sleeping in the University auditorium to protest the new student fees and the whole Bologna process that had re-structured the German University system. Like something was actually happening, like we were having our say.

And because I was lying next to the man I had been crushing on ever since I saw him playing bass in a tiny sweaty club in Duisburg, a city about half an hour away from Bochum. I had accompanied Svenja to the gig and was slightly disappointed to realise afterwards that *he* seemed to be pining for *her*.

Falling in love with someone who loves you back – to this day – seems to me like an impossibility. Like an unsolvable equation: how would that even work?

It had always been a thing for me, every time I wasn't in a relationship, I entered a sort of parallel world of my twenties where I was constantly in unrequited love with someone, sometimes for years. A sort of bi-product to having a writer's brain, I guess. There's always a (love) story to spin.

The word *unrequited* in most dictionaries is related to love, stating that "If the love that you feel for someone is unrequited, it is not felt in the same way by the other person: it's just another poem on the pain of unrequited love."[4]

It seems to disproportionately happen to people with low self-esteem. There is something about seeking negative feedback to confirm the negative esteem you have of yourself. Nathaniel Branden a Canadian-

[4] Cambridge Dictionary, https://dictionary.cambridge.org/dictionary/english/unrequited

American psychotherapist stated in *The Six Pillars of Self-Esteem* that "self-esteem creates a set of implicit expectations about what is possible and appropriate to us", and that "one's reality confirms and strengthens one's original belief".[5]

– Yet I think it is not just about that.

There's something about story-telling that is about control, too. And what else is the nourishing substance of unrequited love? It's the idea, the phantasy, the intense belief, the story we tell ourselves that one day, they will see us in the right way.

The irony is that when that day comes, when they actually do see you, when they're lying next to you on an ugly fibre bonded carpet, that someone chose for its durability so that it will last the many students and professors feet walking over it for decades, that then you might find yourself unable to move or worse, *turning around, facing the metal legs of a table.*

Loving someone from afar is safe. It is only happening within you, within your control.

So I guess, I hate being in love.

---

[5] Branden, Nethaniel *The Six Pillars of Self-Esteem*. Bantam Books 1994

DANCE.

We are down a bottle of wine when the music starts to sound too appealing not to. Not to get up and move. At first, it's just our heads and I don't know why we're suddenly shouting I guess because someone has turned up the volume and some salsa tune is transforming the living room into a beach bar in San Sebastian or Marseille.

Our heads flung high as we howl to Kate Bush's *Wuthering Heights* realising neither of us knows the lyrics properly. We look them up and say in astonishment "Oh it's Heathcliff! Ah that makes sense," but we still use our own made-up gibberish. We are laughing and looking for more, for better tunes that take us back to older versions of ourselves, to parts we usually hide.

Our stupid teenage selves.

The ones that used to want so much, feel so much in the course of a mere 24 hours. With badly applied make-up and very little fabric covering our most important parts, the ill-fated ideas about romance, the rules we proclaimed and broke – every single one of them.

The certainty of being young and enough mistakes lying ahead. The innocence of recklessness. Because there's still so much time to get it right.

– And why do you think there's none now? You're not a finished product ready to be sold. You're not an exponential line chart. You're not a present to give away. You are a work-in-progress for the rest of your life. When you were young, you understood something but you based it on an age, you attached it to a timeline.

When it's all there in that moment, when you get up because you enjoy something, when you move your body because it feels good, the truth you'll always want to hold onto, every breath that you take, every inhale is a new chance, to begin again, to let yourself go, to feel young and vibrant, and *amazingly stupid.*

Parachutes Couldn't Carry Us Higher

2

My dad points something out that I have known most of my life: *there are only women*. He points at the photo in my phone, the one where all my birthday guests sit smiling around a large table in my favourite wine bar.

I often wondered why, for most of my life, I had only female friends apart from gay men and non-binary people. What was it that constantly led me into the arms of female companionship, sisterhood? Was it preference or avoidance? Coincidence or circumstance?

The few times I had a heterosexual male friend it was of a temporary nature often ending when that man entered a new relationship or when the seriousness of that relationship heightened.

In school being friends with boys often meant an unwanted romantic or sexual tension coming from them, so that I simply avoided them altogether. There's only that many times it feels fun to be the object of someone's desire and by that I mean it was never fun. It was actually quite insulting. Why would I waste my energy on forging a friendship with someone that was not actually interested in me as a person? When the condition of that friendship was sexual favours and/or reciprocal romantic feelings, which effectively is the un-definition of friendship.

And the few times when this might not have been the case I was already too scared, too timid to try. The waters of heterosexual friendship felt muddy and sometimes dangerous.

Besides, the experience of living in a female body, the ways in which patriarchy prohibits most men to be vulnerable saddens me, but I just couldn't be bothered.

It's a strange dance to have a close friendship in a heteronormative culture anyway. Girlfriends and wives, boyfriends and husbands whose jealousy can easily seep in and taint the bond of friendship. Or as Sylvia Plath put it once: "My consuming interest in men and their lives is often misconstrued as a desire to seduce them, or as an invitation to intimacy."[6]

Two years ago I wrote on my new year's list: *find a male friend*. I felt that something was wrong with me. Why on earth did I not have one single heterosexual male friend? I could sense what Rebecca Solnit once wrote, "You should be with people who are like you, who dream your dreams and fight your battles, who recognize you. And then, other times, you should be like people unlike yourself. Because there is a problem as well with those who spend too little time being anyone else; it stunts the imagination in which empathy takes root (...)."[7]

It's a quote intended to be about the dominance of the white heterosexual male view in our culture and especially literature, but I think one can transfer that sentiment onto actual real-life contact as well. The same goes for race, class, cultural heritage, not just gender. Staying in one's bubble never did anyone good.

When I looked around, most of my female friends didn't have them either. Male companionship was only ever happening in my life when I met the friends of a boyfriend After the breakup, they would usually dissipate.

---

[6] The Unabridged Journals of Sylvia Plath, 1950-62, Smith College

[7] Rebecca Solnit, Recollections of My Non-Existence, Viking 2020

Finding friends can be difficult in the first place as you get older. Or, more accurately, it's more difficult to find close friends – the only friends I really want. I never cared much for acquaintances.

There's also different understandings of what friendships are, what they offer and how they are navigated. Not everyone wants the kind of friendship I aspire to. They're happy to receive an occasional text to hang out, a short interruption in their busy 9-5 work schedule. Nothing that goes beyond an hour coffee break.

Once I went for dinner in a fancy restaurant with a friend and she felt guilty because she was out fine dining with me instead of with her husband. As if all nice things have to be reserved for a romantic partner. Where abstinence is a love language. In all honesty, something I have absolutely conformed to myself in the past. The anger I have felt when my partner would do something special with another friend, something that I wanted to do as well: the rage of finding out they watched that movie, went to that special restaurant already. The audacity! I am after all a hypocrite, too. But I'm learning.

There's so much insecurity around romantic relationships these days resulting in dogmatic behaviour around what is for romantic relationships and what is for friendships. The second class character of friendship becomes especially apparent when after a breakup the argument is: *why* can't we be friends? As if that was a demotion. As if friendship was a sort of consolation prize.

Once you're not in a romantic relationship navigating holidays and festivities, anything habitual or ritual based turns out to be a difficult parkour of different expectations, norms and actual feelings for each other. Which is why some people are righteously desperate when they do find themselves alone (again). Wouldn't you be? If you're suddenly stripped off all your privileges? The things you didn't have to consider for so long but now do.

The second time I show the birthday photo of my friends to someone it's my sister and, immediately, not knowing what my father had said, she repeats the same. *There are only women.* I wonder if it isn't saying something else, too. When I tell her that most women I know only have female friends, how this is quite common she says, "yes but don't they have boyfriends or partners?"

– They do. But they're not my friends. They're okay but I actually don't know them. Why would I invite people to an intimate champagne and oyster extravaganza and then have to deal with these people I barely know clinging on to the cool people I want to celebrate with. *On my birthday?!*

I don't say this to her as our conversation abruptly ends as, so often when family is around, someone needs something or another question is asked but it stirs me up later during the day.

I don't know how she meant it, if it just has to do with the fact that she has been in a long-term relationship for all of her twenties up to her mid-thirties, and has now been married for seven years, that because she is so used to being in mixed groups for the last fifteen years it just seemed odd to her seeing only women at a birthday party.

But I can't help to feel a slight undercurrent, something that is whispering from the bottom of that comment that says: *incomplete.*

And I desperately want to shake it.

KISSING GIRLS.

I fucking hate men! I shout over the street in the middle of the night as I sit down to pee between two cars. My general peeing spot in the city I declare to my friend. Everyone should have one. It gives you a sense of order at night walking home.

Traffic lights, alley to the right – peeing spot – halfway home.

I grab her hand and we start running, giggling. The sound of our feet tripping on the wet concrete. We're well into our late twenties but tonight we're something else. We're lovers. We are leaning each other into walls / against lampposts/ against cars.

It's long after midnight, in the middle of a dancing crowd and something feels different. Something, mainly you, your eyes look different, like they're about to tell a secret. And I can't wait to hear. You come closer and I try to figure it out. Figure you out. You're shape shifting, bending to the music. Your mouth too close to not give in. I want to. *I really want to.*

Let's do this. You say with your lips touching mine. We laugh. We already are doing it. I bite your lip, you bite back harder. This is everything it should be, I think. And I open my eyes and it should be just you and me. But it isn't just you and me and me and you, there is someone else, too.

Why?
Why?
Why?

Fuck off! I don't even need to hear what his stupid face is about to say. It's the third guy tonight trying to get 'in'. Desperately turned on by what he is seeing, thinking it is for his eyes, his pleasure, him only. That we're doing it for the attention, that this is just a show, a preview, a sample, a snippet, an AD. As if we're just waiting to be released by some dick cutting in.

I'm tired. You say.   And I: let's go home.

We hold hands and you take off your shoes. For a while we don't talk at all. I wonder what is holding you back, what is holding us back now. At the corner we start kissing again. We think we're safe. We should be safe. We're not.

"Why not?" The guy asks, as you shout at him, "No! No! No!" And, "fuck off!" And thank God he is alone and there's people on the street. Your hand in his face. An arm length between you and his idea of a threesome. He doesn't dare to stay any longer and moves on.

Was that too aggressive? You ask and I shake my head.

Was that too aggressive? You ask again.

And I kiss you. And I kiss you again.

No. It was just enough. Just the right amount. *Just right.*

And you smile and we walk in silence. All the way home and we –

don't kiss anymore.

Parachutes Couldn't Carry Us Higher

3

Memory is *lacunose*, filled with gaps like an ancient text some parts lost to the erosion of time. A *lacuna* from Latin "a ditch, pit; a hollow, cavity; a gap, defect" meaning "an absent part, especially in a book or other piece of writing."[8] The empty spaces where something should be, lost due to the selectiveness and capacity of our brains to contain information.

There is beauty in that, the poetry of Sappho for instance, the poetess of the ancient Greece, whose œvre today only exists in fragments that almost shine brighter in their elusiveness. Though their yearning can sometimes feel inconclusive about the true meaning, the real intent.

[8] https://en.wiktionary.org/wiki/lacuna

As a writer I am used to filling these gaps with story, pouring one letter after the other into the little cavities in my mouth.

My therapist asks me to write a letter to my dad. I'm reluctant. I say: *I've already been through this*. I had this whole talk with him, five, six years ago. Surely there is a time limit on childhood trauma. Surely there must be a lid you can put on it. At some point. I guess this is how far talking can get you.

How far writing can get you. The body keeps the score, unfortunately. Is it a scar or still an open wound?

I don't write the letter.

Sometimes what seems like a cavity is really an abyss where words go to drown.

—

When I was twelve years old my pet rabbit died. I found her alone, coming home after school, walking through the garden, passing the rabbit cage like I always did. Looking inside like I always did, thinking: oh, she's sleeping. And then realising that she was stiff, lifeless, dead.

I cried for an hour, sitting in the grass in front of the wooden shed my dad had built, watching my sister's rabbit downstairs, still alive hopping from one corner to the other. I had forgotten my key and waited for my mum to come home.

Hysterical, that's how I remember her. Mixing up the names of the rabbits, moving her hands around rapidly like a headless chicken. My dad found me later, hiding under the covers of my bed, sat beside me, stroked my hair, and said nothing.

The next day at school I would tell the story of how my dad had been there for me, exactly the way I needed it and then later on, as I grew older this story would grow too and evolve into the moment I knew my dad actually cared about me. *Memory is also talismanic.* And I held onto this one tightly.

There's another moment: I was an extra in a musical, a soldier, when I was about the same age, maybe a bit older. For ten minutes I had to stand on stage, guarding the crowning ceremony of *The Pauper and the Prince*. Because I was tall and soldiers are men and men are tall, or so went the logic back then, I was cast for the role. About four or five minutes into the scene I started wobbling. The heat of summer, the bright hot lights, the excitement, the costume, the helmet: it all was wearing me down. Standing on the edge of the stage my dad, observing my pale white face, jumped out of the audience, raced through the corridor, and caught me right before I fell, dragging me behind the stage.

I think my dad liked being a hero. He would be the kind of father who would rush me to the hospital when I accidentally jumped into shards of glass. He was there when he could do something. Build something. When he knew what and how to do it. When he could be strong.

—

Just as.

I have never seen my dad cry.

I remember once he did but secretly on a very rare occasion while we were watching *American History X*, just me and him sitting in the living room, waiting for my mum to come home, I must have been seventeen or eighteen and all of my siblings had moved out already and somehow this movie was on TV that night and because my dad is a *serious man* and this is a *serious movie* I thought the two would match.

I did not quite anticipate the explicit brutality that would be displayed in the film, the horrors of white supremacy, that one scene, if you've watched the movie, you know exactly what I am talking about, a pavement, a kick, a crack. But the last thing I expected was my dad's reaction.

"Your dad was completely destroyed last night." My mum told me the next morning over breakfast. "It really hit him. What kind of movie were you watching?" she added with an accusing tone, as if I should have known, "Your dad is a very *sensitive man*."

– This was news to me.

The first man that I saw crying was my first boyfriend. I remember it very vividly because I did not handle it well. At all. In fact I acted horribly. At first I wouldn't say anything, then I would flinch or roll my eyes and at some point, I think I am not exactly sure but I might have burst out with the words: "oh my god, can you please stop whining!"

There are always moments you'd wish you could rewind and change when it comes to relationships and this is absolutely one of them.

–

In my early twenties, I had the opportunity to be one of the chosen people that got a job as an assistant at the prestigious *Burgtheater* in Vienna, a theatre dubbed in the German-speaking realm as "one of the best". It had been during my Erasmus semester and by sheer coincidence I landed a job for a two-month production of the play *The Commune* directed by Thomas Vinterberg.

One evening after rehearsal, Vinterberg, one of the actors and I walked back to the tram station. They were heavily discussing a problem that occurred during rehearsal and, being a 20-year-old, I constantly felt out of place, I trotted along not really contributing to anything. *I might as well not be here*, I thought, and when the time came and my tram arrived I didn't feel like interrupting their flow so I just got on after whispering goodbye, but I'm quite sure neither of them heard it.

The next morning when I was making myself a coffee Vinterberg stood behind me, tapped on my shoulder, and said, "I'm awfully sorry about yesterday, about not having said goodbye. You were all of a sudden gone and I guess we were too focused on the discussion. That shouldn't have happened. I'm sorry."

There are people who see you even when you don't see yourself.

–

"All of humanity's problems stem from man's inability to sit quietly in a room alone,"[9] wrote the French philosopher Blaise Pascal. Which I think to a degree is true, but I would argue that a lot of other problems stem from a man's inability to be vulnerable and thus to connect with others. Because most of the time we are not alone in the room. There are others. There are always others. Even when you conceal all your emotions and bottle them up and keep them in your head and pretend you're all alone in this world. You're not.

This year Vinterberg won an Oscar for his film *Another Round.* Originally titled *Druk* meaning: drinking yourself into a coma. The film is about four "deprived, white, drunk men," he said in his Oscar speech, who all work as teachers at the same high school.

In one of the first scenes, we see Martin, played by the wonderful Mads Mikkelsen, sitting at the table in a fancy restaurant, trying to pull it together. It's his friend Nikolaj's birthday, and the four men talk about how things are at school at the moment, their family lives, how Martin seems to be having trouble with his class. His apathy towards life worries everyone. They persuade him to have a drink even though he refused before because he is driving.

[9] Blaise Pascal, Pensées, 1669-70

As Martin is chugging down the alcohol a transition is made that is watering his eyes, tears welling up, eyelids flicker, he cannot contain it, cannot hold his own anymore. Only with alcohol as the catalyst, he can reveal himself. He cries and immediately apologises for it "Sorry," he says, as if his tears were an attack.

And I want to tell him that he shouldn't be sorry and I wish one of them would get up and hug him and say that but his friends, though empathetically looking at him, do what probably most men do in these situations; divert the conversation and try to cheer him up. It's then when I realise how much I have longed to see a man cry on screen. For the sheer reason that his wife isn't really talking to him, admitting that he is lonely and he doesn't know what to do. *Like a normal person. With emotions.*

– Actual male fragility and I want to see it.

As the film goes on and alcohol takes the centre stage in the process of the four men letting go of their lives, I do wonder what would happen if these men went to therapy. Or if they actually started talking about their feelings when they're not drunk. Because you can sense that their friendship is real. They take care of each other, they genuinely care. But they are also trapped in a society that wants them to *man up!*

Alcohol is the only love language they know. A language that is slowly drowning them. And we all know these men. They're our fathers, our grandfathers, our brothers, our teachers, our bosses, our partners, men who would rather hide in a dark room than be seen as vulnerable by someone that cares for them. With all the privileges and power that they have been provided by the patriarchy, being a human that is allowed to display the whole range of emotions is somehow not one of them.

– At the end of Vinterberg's Oscar speech, he talks about the death of his daughter Ida, dedicating the film to her. She died in a car accident, at the same time when Vinterberg had just started shooting his film. He is very composed as he talks about it, but then he wipes a tear from his cheek, and his voice breaks as he mutters: sorry.

This morning I asked my dad if he realises that I never saw him cry during my childhood. The question hovers weirdly above us.

Were you sad? Were you scared? Were you hurt? Were you lonely? Could you feel it?

– *Could you show it?*

I could hear him shifting, changing his tone from formal to funny. *I don't know*, he said finally. I do sometimes cry when I watch a sad movie. And we both laugh and I let it go. Change cannot happen overnight. Trust cannot be built in a minute of compassion when there has been a lifetime of damage. It's an ongoing conversation. A question at the beginning. A start.

Till then I hold this space.

I almost cried.

– *I wish you had.*

It's strange how you never see it coming.

Even when you do.

How the things you loved suddenly turn into patterns, shifting your perspective to tell a new story, a different one from the one you told yourself before.

How every heartbreak is about the prehistoric wound.

It's time to tell that story.

It's time to summon ghosts.

For the longest time I had forgotten what happened. Forgotten that it actually had happened. To me. While that is actually not true, I just hadn't thought about it. Or talked about it. The words could not find a place to land.

I hadn't bothered to look. Like a forgotten cupboard under the stairs: I knew it was there. A vague recollection of events. But just like stuffing everything with no home inside a drawer as you go through your day, it was unconscious, it wasn't because I thought it was right to put it there, that it belonged. It just didn't feel that important. It simply had no place to be anywhere else.

What didn't occur to me then, was that it was making its rounds at night, how it determined my behaviour, how it shaped my relationships, how I viewed myself, how it actually wasn't in the cupboard at all, but spreading like termites in the floorboards. Slowly eroding, weakening the substance.

—

We often slept over at my grandmother's house when I was little. Sometimes it would just be me, sometimes my sister would join, or my cousins. Up in the attic, three little rooms that had once belonged to my dad and his two siblings.

One of my favourite memories is carefully climbing down the steep stairs early in the morning, opening the wooden door to the kitchen and finding my grandmother already up and about, pouring me a cold *Kakao,* leaving little lumps in the milk, that I loved to eat up with an old silver spoon that was shaped like a seashell. It was the only thing I asked for when my parents were clearing her house after she died.

I think it was then, lying in his old bed, that I was picturing my dad for the first time as a little boy who played just like me in the hidden corners, watching everything from the oval window over the courtyard. The realisation that he, too, had a childhood. Hearing the creaking sounds of the wooden beams at night, the rain on the tiles so much closer, the heavy down duvet to keep warm and the cold in the morning seeping in through the roof. These rooms had been filled with life and memories, with excitement and joy and fights over toys and, once, with a guinea pig that was disguised as a hamster because my grandmother had forbidden bigger rodents in the house.

My dad was born in 1958, the eldest of three children. There's not a lot I know about his childhood. He was a left-hander who was forced in school to write with his right hand which made his handwriting indecipherable. He only went to school till he was fifteen. He had a funny looking haircut like everyone in the 60s. He helped out in his parent's coal and drink delivery business after school. And of course the "hamster".

–

Why don't you love me?

I'm ten and my dad sits opposite of me and is speechless. He often is deliberately. But this time for various reasons he doesn't know how to answer this. Maybe because there is no real answer to this question and he knows that. Nothing can answer this question right. Because *this question* should never exist in the first place. This whole situation is absurd.

Yet I am sitting there, insisting.

Why don't you love me?

Sixteen years later I will sit there again, insisting. In a different setting, this time in Berlin. My dad and my mum are on my couch in the living room. I'm struggling at University but really I am just struggling with life. Surrounded by ghosts. This time asking a different question. The one that had always been lying underneath.

"Why did you hit me?"

He says nothing.

Surrounded by ghosts, it's scary to speak.

–

It's Christmas Eve and I'm alone with my parents. My siblings are all married with children, have their own, new traditions in their own, new homes and will arrive in the next days to come. My mother is sitting on the couch, writing someone a text message while my dad is in the kitchen, preparing our dinner. Twenty years ago it probably would have been the other way around, but everything has changed since then.

Some traditions stick though, so we watch *Emil of Lönneberga* for the hundredth time. A much-loved classic children's movie based on the book series written by Astrid Lindgren, a Swedish children's author who was, and still is, very popular in Germany.

Emil is a little boy living on a farm around the year 1900 in Småland, Sweden. Famous in the local village for his ingenious pranks and wit, he gets shoved into the shed almost on the daily by his mother, when his father, frequently enraged with fury from his pranks, wants to beat him.

The door of Emil's shed has two locks, one on the inside so that Emil's father cannot come in, and one on the outside so that Emil can't get out. It's an arrangement that works for both of them. His father can cool his temper and Emil learns to like being in the shed, as he uses the time to work on his wood carving figurines, which fill the shed like talismans of all of his pranks.

The title of prankster is quite misleading regarding Emil, as most of the things he does stem from an eager curiosity, a children's logic or just a misunderstanding. He never does anything to belittle or to demean or to make fun of anybody. It's Lindgren's special way of storytelling that understands the point of view of children, leading to sympathise with her child protagonists and to highlight the injustice they're often faced with from their caretakers.

I think of the shed as a symbol of safety. A haven far away from violence. The fact that Emil could close that door. Lock it. Shut his parents out.

—

When you're a child and you have to explain to yourself that the person who is supposed to love you, supposed to care for you, when that person hurts you, so much that you're afraid of them afterwards, that you fear the footsteps coming up the stairs and the door swinging open because you've been fighting with your sister or you were loud or you don't even remember what it was because it was nothing and to know that no pleading, no crying, will help, when that irrational force is entering your life, harming your body and there is no door to shut, nothing to protect you, when this person an hour later is sitting with you at the dinner table, casually talking to you about your day, *there must be a way to excuse that.*

Something is created then. A cognitive dissonance. A split. In order to sit at that table and believe that my dad actually was my dad, the person that *took care of me*, I needed to invent something. The first ghost: that to be loved doesn't mean you're safe. That in order to be loved, pain is not only inevitable. It's part of it.

And you're not allowed to protect yourself.

You just have to take it.

–

Growing up in the 90s, I am part of the last generation to be corporally punished legally, meaning that any form of disciplinary act of physical violence was allowed as long as it did not leave marks, as long as there was no use of weapons or objects. I was lucky in the sense that, like most of the people my age that I ever talked to about this, I was never hit beyond the lawful limit. It only happened a few times. I was maybe five or six or seven. Maybe eight. It's hard to put a timeline on this as I don't remember exactly. *Memory is lacunose.* My father doesn't remember either. But we both do know that it happened.

–

It is no surprise to me that when I tell my father how I am going to write about this, to shine a light on this issue how it shaped so much of my behaviour, he still doesn't see anything *really* wrong with it. *What was I supposed to do?* He felt provoked, helpless, he didn't know how else to react. He tells me on the phone. My father is really bad at apologising.

In the background, my mother shouts, "your dad is sorry." And then, to him this time, urging "tell her!"

Maybe he is. Maybe he isn't.

Maybe this is not about him.

Maybe I hold space for him to change.

But more importantly this time I am holding space for myself.

And what I believe in.

—

A shift in German culture and knowledge about the damaging effects on children's psychology and their wellbeing would lead to eventually banning all physical and psychological violence against children in 1998 and be written into a law in 2000.

Yet there's still a language and a culture around *spanking, slapping, smacking* that always makes it sound like the violence used was sort of mild and harmless. Sentiments like: it didn't really hurt. Or: I was a terrible child, I deserved it. Or worse: I needed a good spanking sometimes. They paint a picture of violence being an integral part to secure and shape a child's good character. A belief so ancient and deeply rooted it is found in almost all cultures.

"Only 14% of the world's children are fully protected in law from all corporal punishment."[10] In England, the U.S., and in many other countries it is still, to this day, lawful to discipline your own children with some version of corporal punishment. Often citing what amounts to a "reasonable punishment" according to section 58 of the Children Act 2004. Any punishment above what is considered "reasonable" is illegal. Scotland, where I reside, banned it just recently in 2020. Wales implemented a ban in 2022.

We are all a bit late. And we all need to stop pretending it's not a symptom of larger issues. Or that just because a country bans it, people stop immediately. *Violence feeds violence.* A society which teaches

[10] https://endcorporalpunishment.org/

children that it's alright to receive violence and to use violence when you're an adult against a child, shows that our most vulnerable aren't protected like everyone else is. That children do not deserve the same rights in the regard of safety and well-being as adults. What kind of society does that project?

And how do we repair the bonds impaired or broken of the last generations before it was banned? What about that transitional time? The ones in-between.

"We all desire peace. So is there any possibility at all of our changing fundamentally, before it's too late? Of our learning to distance ourselves from violence? Of our trying quite simply to become a new kind of human beings? But how could we go about that, and where should we start? I believe that we should start from the bottom. With the children." said Astrid Lindgren in her speech *Never violence!* upon receiving the Peace Prize of the German Book Trade in 1978.[11]

The speech sounds so contemporary, it could be given, word for word, today. "No wonder we are all afraid, whether we belong to a great power or live in a small neutral country. We all know that another world war will not spare any of us, and whether I am buried under a neutral or non-neutral pile of rubble should make little difference. After these millennia of constant wars, don't we have to ask ourselves whether humans are perhaps already flawed from within? Are we doomed because of our aggression?"[12]

In it she describes the story of a young mother who wants to discipline her child. She orders him to go out and find a stick, so she can whip him. After a long time the little boy comes, back with a stone in his hand crying and in sheer agony. He puts the stone on the table and apologises to her, because he wasn't able to find a stick however he thought she could use this stone to throw it at him. That is the moment the young mother realises what she had done and what she wasn't going to do anymore. She hugged her little boy and put the stone on the kitchen cupboard as a reminder to never use violence again.

---

[11] Transl. of *Niemals Gewalt!* Astrid Lindgren's acceptance speech of Peace Prize of the German Book Trade, 1978

[12] Transl. of *Niemals Gewalt!* Astrid Lindgren's acceptance speech German Peace Prize of the German Book Trade, 1978

—

At 26 I confronted my dad for the first time, because I suddenly remembered. Because it felt like the termites had eroded everything, my substance, and I was wading through the remnants of myself. He crumbled, too.

Suddenly like a wee boy sitting in front of me, he said: "do you know how my dad hit me? Right in the face. And I am not complaining."

That's when I knew. He could never apologise. To accept that violence is wrong, to hold himself accountable, he would have to dismiss a whole narrative of being at war with the world, of what his father represented, society. It would have cost him too much.

—

People will go to great lengths to protect their stories. But I'm afraid I'm done with that. This story has multiple beginnings, but it has no end. It has no solution, but continuous communication. Just like every story, it is more about what is not said, than what is. Memory is lacunose, but so is speech. Those visible gaps that I'm still trying to fill.

Joan Didion wrote in her famous essay collection *The White Album,* "we tell ourselves stories to live"[13] but I think I tell myself stories to confuse myself, to cover up the things I don't want to know, which I would argue is a way of surviving, not living.

"Sometimes I like my dad a lot, sometimes I don't," says Emil to his friend, the farmhand Alfred. It's interesting how it never occurred to me to just dismiss my dad like that. To just hate how he treated me and be done with it. I would *write* in my diary how much I hated him when I was a child but it never stuck. I always looked for affection from men that were clearly incapable of giving.

"Why don't you love me?" I asked back then. A ten year old, sitting next to fish, swirling. Nowadays I sometimes go back to that memory and change it. I play out a different version, one where I'm building a

[13] Joan Didion, The White Album, Simon Schuster, 1979

shed inside of me. A protective realm. Where I say: I don't care about you. And this is not working for me. So I'm going to leave.

When I was a child, I didn't have anywhere to go. As children we depend on our caretakers to love us and we will do anything to achieve that love. Even when we have to invent ghosts.

And when you're grown up.

You need to stop believing in them.

—

The essayist Fariha Róisín wrote at the age of 33, the same age I am now, "I'm learning there's a self I want to protect."[14] All my life I have been protecting others and their careless behaviour, in a strange attempt to also protect myself. A pattern I learned from my ghosts. All behaviour is in a way self-preserving no matter how dysfunctional it may seem. But that thing I was protecting wasn't really me. It was the story I told myself about that person that I didn't want to let go of. The idea, the hope I had for us. People go to great lengths to not be wrong about something.

But I was wrong. So many times.

I'm learning there's a self I want to protect.

[14] https://fariharoisin.substack.com/p/another-year-another-becoming

Things I Have Loved

I want you to think of me dancing
(eyes closed
limbs flung all over and under
my chin up
so high)
solivagant
I catch shooting stars in my hair

The Lost Empress

1

At first I lost *Temperance*. It was during a very hot summer in Paris, a sudden gust of wind and there she was, lying in the rain gutters of the silvery blue metal rooftops that Paris is so famous for.

It seemed quite fitting that she was down there now. Looking up at me with two golden cups in her hand pouring one into the other, her flaming red wings spread wide. Out of reach, yet I could still read the lettering.

It seemed like a sign, like life was trying to tell me something. That things were out of balance, out of line. That my feet needed to touch the ground again. I had just graduated finishing a four year course in playwriting at the University of Arts in Berlin. Ahead of me was a long train journey through the south of France and Italy, to arrive three weeks later in Sicily to attend a wedding.

It was a summer of abundance, extravagant dinners and wine, a summer to make grand decisions and radical life changes. My Saturn return. It was then that I decided, walking on a dusty street towards a tiny chapel somewhere in the hills of Petralia, to finally leave Berlin behind me.

If life could look like this, what was I *doing*?

It was a time I still refer to as *that brief moment where I had a lot of money*, where I could just afford going out to restaurants all the time, where a taxi home was not a headache, buying snacks on the go, where I could book a holiday without thinking too much about costs. A life that for a majority of people is absolutely normal and that most would not call *rich* at all. Perhaps lower-middle class. I still have a weird relationship with money, it does not feel real to me. I am joyously ignorant about saving. I don't understand how two meals out and a grocery shop totals up to a hundred pounds. I am constantly surprised when things add up and how. It all feels made up to me, in part because, of course, *it is*.

I try very hard to change that, to understand the cost of living. To understand when I need to say no and to save money for the next month. And to also understand when saving is not even an option. When I can barely make ends meet.

—

Losing *Temperance* made sense, for a while. After all, it was urging me to seek it. To focus on it. The mind loves to think of the things it has lost. It's drawn to them like a black hole. It made me reconfigure. What was important to me. What needed to be put back into balance. What was too much for me to take.

It's funny how not all things are lost immediately, but over time. Not everything is rushed off with the wind. How long it sometimes takes to notice that something's actually missing.

Eventually, to continue using the tarot deck, I replaced *Temperance* with a blank card. Always reminding me when it came up of that moment in Paris on the balcony, that summer. I wonder if she's still up there; if a pigeon took her or the rain wore her down. Slowly disintegrating.

The mind loves to think of the things it has lost.

I've always used tarot cards as a means to understand myself better, a sort of prettier Rorschach test, letting my mind dive into the imagery and attach it to certain aspects, words, bouncing off of feelings, reflections of the state of mind I was in.

The ritual of drawing a card when I'm uncertain, holding a prophecy in my hand, an oracle. And just like all oracles only in hindsight seeing a clearer picture, a narrative. The major arcana telling a story, a journey that starts or ends with *the Fool*. Of all things, it is *the Fool* dancing at the edge of a cliff, looking up at the sun, bravely and blissfully walking through life. A symbol of mortality reminding us that we're constantly dancing on the edge, as no one knows their death date. No one knows how much time they have. But still dancing. Still brave. What a marvellous concept to make meaning of the chaos that is everyday life.

It's funny how not all things are lost immediately, but over time. How long it sometimes takes to notice that something's actually missing.

It made sense to me when I decided to stay in Edinburgh to choose *the Empress* as my guiding star. She represents divine femininity, intuition, strength, creativity. Qualities I was longing for. I remember how I placed her on the window sill in my new home. How I draped sunflowers and peonies I had found on the street around her, it felt fitting to eternalise this moment in a photo. Looking back now:

– It was the last time I saw her.

BOOKS.

It's spring without you. It's the green leaves emerging and the air tasting like fresh cut cucumbers: moist, cold, pure. I want to put them in a gin and tonic to drown.

I walk by a bookshop and find a used version of Marcelle Sauvageot's *Laissez-moi: Commentaire*. I pay 4€ and read it the whole afternoon at *Schillerpark*. The lilacs are slouching forward, filling the air with their rich sweet scent. I break off a few branches to bring home.

Sauvageot wrote letters to her ex-lover, her ex-fiancé, while impatiently trying to heal from tuberculosis and a broken heart at a Sanatorium in 1930. She never sends them. Instead, encouraged by a friend, she publishes them. Writing about real people is always cruel. They don't have a chance to answer.

So I guess this is revenge.

3 years later. At 27. Another spring. Another you. Another broken heart. I remember Sauvageot. And I write it all down. All those you's. All of it. The whole Heartbreak Hotel. I decorate the rooms. I turn them into one. I call it *This Feeling Of Emptiness Like Shopping For Groceries And Forgetting To Bring The Pfandflaschen*.

I merge her words and mine, I put them into the mouth of an actress. She walks on stage, dripping wet, explaining our grief.

I never talk to you again. I publish everything instead.

—

I'm in Edinburgh and the light is getting weaker. It's November and I'm coming to terms with the fact that living alone sucks. And I cannot afford it.

This is where she finds me. I open the first page of *Things I don't want to know* by Deborah Levy, standing there in the bookshop something else opens. Levy writes how she is crying on escalators, how in all places, her body and mind seem to choose that one. Me on my own mental escalator at that time, her words lift me up. It feels like talking to Deborah Levy. As if.

—

I'm at my parent's home watching a tv program and the landscape of Orkney, Scotland flickering over the screen along with a tall blond woman watching birds sets that longing slowly awakening again to leave Berlin and my old life behind. To find something else, something different. Something *like that.*

I don't remember exactly how and when I read Amy Liptrot's *The Outrun,* but it must have been around the same time I was decluttering my memory chest, an old wooden family heirloom, the dowry of a great-great-aunt from 1892. I had made the decision to move to Edinburgh and it felt quite fitting to read a memoir by a Scottish author who was more or less my age.

I remember sitting on the floor with conflicting feelings about my teens and early twenties, contemplating how I actually wanted to live my life and justifying a move, while reading about the struggles of another, guiding me towards myself.

—

New York in early fall and a spartanic Airbnb in Bushwick. It's my first time in the city having overcome my inherent and ongoing fear of flying. I walk a lot and subsequently am tired a lot. I find out that a poet is renting the bunk bed next to me. It's a four-bed dorm and at 3am the guy underneath me doesn't realise his headphones aren't plugged in properly and we can all hear the soothing voice of Ira Glass hosting another podcast episode of *This American Life* till someone musters up the courage to let him know.

The poet and I exchange Instagram handles, the next day we watch the presidential debates and everybody is still hoping that Hillary will win. Months later I see a book popping up on the poet's Instagram page: *Spinster* by Kate Bolick. Newly heartbroken and single, I trust her advice and order my own copy the same day.

"Being single is like being an artist, not because creating a functional single life is an art form, but because it requires the same close attention to one's singular needs, as well as the will and focus to fulfill them. Just as the artist arranges her life around her creativity, sacrificing conventional comforts and even social acceptance, sleeping and eating according to her own rhythms, so that her talent thrives above all else, nurtured the way a child might be, so a single person has to think hard to decipher what makes her happiest and most fulfilled."[15]

Bolick writes about her personal path as a spinster, while also describing other women's fates. Specifically, other women who wrote: columnist Neith Boyce, essayist Maeve Brennan, social visionary Charlotte Perkins Gilman, poet Edna St. Vincent Millay, and novelist Edith Wharton.

Watching her, watching other women, trying to find connections, weaving ourselves into the narration. I read about Wharton and end up on *Les Iles d'Or - Porquerolles,* a French island, two years later. Wharton had been resident in a glamorous little hotel, where I would also take up a room.

I would wander around the island in the hot August sun, find hidden pools with fewer people, dive into the clear turquoise water, sit on the rocky cliffs and take that day with me, the heat, the smell of oranges and thyme, the air underneath my armpits racing down the hill on a bicycle I rented.

Books do exactly that. They lead you places. They connect you to the world, to yourself, if you let them.

---

[15] Kate Bolick, Spinster

Virginia Woolf once wrote in *Night and Day* (an under-appreciated novel of hers and, personally, my favourite), "there are some books that LIVE (...) They are young with us, and they grow old with us."[16]

[16] Virginia Woolf, Night and Day, 1919 Duckworth

The Lost Empress

2

I thought I had understood. After all I had written a list, I had said *No* and made plans. A vision: I knew what I wanted and was out there to get it.

I was so sure about this. I told the story, my personal gospel. *This is how you do it.* I would tell my single friends. This is the key to finding love.

The worst part is not being clueless. The worst part is thinking you're wise.

And now I talk to a woman at a party and she tells me how she is not dating anyone who talks about *finances* on the first date.

"He told me how he was in debt.

And it made me feel weird that someone would talk about that on a first date."

And now I am 21 and googling *How to know when to break up?*

And now I am 27, it's 3am and I can't sleep and his phone is turned off.

And now I am 32 and it's 3am and I can't sleep and his phone is turned off and I know how this will end. Standing on a beach thinking, "no matter what happens, this will always be here."

And now I am lying in a bed, my nose pressed against someone's neck, thinking this should be forever.

And now it's not.

And I think the red flag is not what someone is particularly doing but how it makes us feel: weird, hurt, sad, desperate, insane, lonely.

There's a distrust concerning the validity of your feelings when you're having low self-worth. Somehow it's not sufficient to draw conclusions from that. You need another reason attached to it. A rule. I'm allowed to feel hurt because ____ It's not enough that *you* feel hurt. There needs to be a validating factor to prove that how you're feeling and thus your reaction is *appropriate*. An excuse. Who taught you this?

I know this is inherently about self-worth and options. And somewhere there I have collected lies, things that aren't true about how much you should be handling: *it should never be this hard to love someone.*

I know this now. But what I wish is to hold onto that, to not forget, to demand more, if anything. Being loved is not a trade-off for how lovable you esteem yourself to be. How much compassion I was willing to give to the other person and the excuses that I made for them, the allowances. *All those ghost stories I made up to conceal the truth.* And how harshly I judged myself in contrast, how seldom I let myself get away with things. The imbalance of that.

On a gloomy Saturday afternoon I walk through the Talbot Rice Gallery with a flashlight that projects ultraviolet light. It's the first solo exhibition of the Chinese artist Qiu Zhijie, who describes himself as a "mapper," encompassing his many professions as a teacher, poet, artist, curator, thinker, researcher and writer.

I point the flashlight at one of the large maps from his Art of War series, hanging on the wall. The maps are covered in Chinese calligraphy, stemming from various important military texts from China, in fluorescent lilac beneath each the English translation shimmers. One line strikes deep and I jot it down in my phone: "Make the enemy unable to judge the situation!"[17]

– Was I the enemy?

---

[17] Exhibition Qiu Zhijie, Talbot Rice Gallery, 2022

On my way home, I take the longer route along the Union Canal, the early setting November sun colouring the water a bright yellow, pondering on the exhibition. Pat Benatar in my head repeatedly preaching *Love is a battlefield.*

To be able to judge a situation, one needs to see clearly, one needs to have enough information. Looking back at my relationships it seemed that they had all scribbled things down, truths in magic marker, hidden messages, in the landscape of my memory, that I was just beginning to see.

Nothing in your life will change if you keep looping on low self-worth.

The Empress wears twelve stars in her crown, showing her connection with the mystical realm and the cycles of the natural world. Her robe is patterned with pomegranates, the fateful fruit that Persephone eats down in the underworld, that tie her to stay with Hades for six months every year thus creating the seasons summer and winter. On a cushion stitched is the symbol of Venus, the planet of love, creativity, fertility, beauty and grace.

Without noticing I had laid tarot cards for two years, with *the Empress* absent. Her wisdom and charisma, somewhere lost between moving houses, between my longing and what I thought I deserved.

Looking at the setting sun, the water now shimmering in fluorescent lilac sending messages from the deep unknown: it was time to find her again.

VIENNA.

It had not been my first choice. It had been more a matter of convenience that I ended up in the winding streets and slow paced grandeur that is Vienna.

Initially I had wanted to go to Edinburgh for a semester abroad but again having missed deadlines, a general unenthusiastic outlook on the support my University showcased and a lack of funds on my part, that path would be delayed for another decade. The promise I had made on Calton Hill, when I was 18 years old, *to return, would have to wait.*

In many ways, in the big ways really, my life has always been a matter of a second try.

Yet Vienna is the place where big things happened. I wrote and staged my second play, a sort of monologue, about Dorothy Parker. It was the setting for eating *Käsekrainer* at night and of friendship bonds that last till today. Of staying whole days in cosy coffee houses, starting with a *soda zitron* and ending with several spritzers till early in the morning. Where there was always time for a *Kaffee* and every syllable of it was pronounced slowly till the end.

In Vienna I learned what it means to *tachinieren,* a lovely untranslatable word whose origins are not exactly certain. It could stem from Austrian military jargon or possibly from the word *Tacherner* which means idler. That would make sense as to be idle is a similar sentiment. I always thought it comes from the word *Tag,* which means day and is also sometimes pronounced as *Tach* in German dialect. That it would allude to the fact that you are just taking the day, doing nothing, merely existing, enjoying yourself. Which in a real way is the true meaning of the word *tachinieren* anyway.

But most importantly it is the place I decided to become a professional writer.

I remember it distinctly after a talk with a friend I had met there, who also was a painter. We often would meet with a couple of other artists in the Viennese parks and paint outside on large cardboards that we would scour from supermarkets nearby. In the lovely May sun, watching people watching us paint she said: *Not like a housewife you know? Do it properly. Take it seriously.*

Of course there's a certain misogynist sentiment underlying this statement. Why housewives? Why not just amateurs? I guess because it speaks of the stereotype of women in their 40s going on artist retreats in Tuscany, painting flowers on silk scarfs, trying to retrieve something. In all honesty, I see nothing wrong with that. *I would love to do that.* But there's an entrapment of housewives. An overload of work that is chronically undervalued. And all these hidden wishes or forsaken paths. And there's the reality, that you *can't* have it all. That is not about being a housewife, that could be working a 9-5 job that you hate, a toxic relationship.

Because what she really meant was: you must choose. Don't half-ass it. Don't take up too many other obligations, focus on this. Do it right. Don't let life just happen to you, don't let the thing that you actually want to do, be reduced to a weekend workshop in Italy.

– So I didn't.

The Lost Empress

3

I'm sitting on the steps of a church somewhere between Gernika and Bilbao watching the heavy rain drops fall onto the asphalt. It's the first time in a week that I am completely walking alone and I'm cherishing the solitude of not being attached to anything but my own body for a moment.

Whatever the *Camino* will bring me I will accept, a promise I gave myself at the beginning of this journey.

So far it has brought me a lovely hiking companion for the first six days, great dinners in *albergues* with other pilgrims, lots of *pintxos* and incredibly affordable wine, a tote bag that I needed and found in a free box, and a feeling of being in tune with myself: a certainty that I am exactly where I am supposed to be right now.

Pilgrims of all kinds walk on the different *Camino's* every year, some friendly, some frustrated, some tired, some looking for connection, some critical, some inspiring, some who I have yet to meet. With every step we choose to go towards something and away from something else, everyone can decide what that is.

The magic lies in recognising that each time.

—

"What are you doing?" – "Waiting for a sign." I sit at a bus stop in Orinión ready to give up when Sophie, another pilgrim, is walking towards me. It's 10.30am, and I have already walked for one and a half hours only to arrive in the same place again.

Orinión – my hell hole, I call it. A little village by the sea, encompassed by tall rocky hills, a cul-de-sac of a place. Last night I had been wandering the beach all by myself looking at the stars, the milky way, I had marvelled at their beauty, now I feel lost, frustrated, trapped.

I have been hiking for 12 days now. Waking up early but not as early as some pilgrims who are gone every morning before I even open my eyes. Packing my little rucksack, deciding which of the two trousers I am going to wear, estimating the temperature, possible rain. Everything has become a ritual: filling up my two water bottles; finding a nice local bakery or cafe to make a proper lunch package for later.

—

I'm lying naked on a beach in Laredo, no one in sight, feeling the warmth of the October sun. Just me and the sound of waves crashing. Just me and a deep gratitude. Just me and everything I have been carrying for two weeks, lying on the sand around me.

Every single thing, every object has its purpose, there is nothing frivolous here, it is all calculated, these are the things I need right now. Anything would be missed if it got lost.

—

Maybe this is the last orange I will ever eat, I think, and bite into the juicy flesh as I look at Sophie and the steep trail. It's not a trail really, more a formation of rocks we are about to climb up. *Los Ojos del Diablo*, the Devil's Eyes is the name of the path we are taking to get over the hill to Laredo. To get out of Orinión and out of the misery I felt down there which I have now exchanged with excitement and a slight fear of having chosen the hill I am going to die on.

When I was packing for the Camino, I had been looking for *the Empress*. I wanted to take something with me, a reminder, a talisman really, that wouldn't take up too much space yet be sentimental enough to work its magic. It was then when I realised that she must have been missing for a while now. That I had laid my fortune without her guiding presence. And in a very real way, it formed a metaphor for what had happened to me: How I had lost my power without even noticing.

In the end I chose *Strengths* to accompany me on my journey. A card that portrays a woman taming a lion, holding his had, his mouth wide open in her hands. Looking up at the hill, it was exactly what I needed to do. Staring into the lion's mouth.

Mach' langsam. "Take your time." I hear my mother's voice in my head with every single step, every rock that I touch, holding onto them, pulling myself up, the heavy rucksack pushing down, trying to not lose my balance: I am literally bear hugging the rock, on all fours. *I love you, rock,* I whisper.

Another pilgrim cried, when she was up here. Sophie told me before. When we were sitting safely in the cafe, me sipping a *ColaCao* and her drinking a *cafe con leche*. I know I can do this. I encourage myself. I have been hiking before, in Bavaria and Austria when I was younger, with my family. This is not even a real mountain. I'm not afraid. I decide.

It's cold and quiet in the church. The golden altar shining brightly, its decorum illuminates the air, this early morning. Me and my roommate for the night have decided to go to the morning prayer with the nuns. I am not religious, but spiritually I feel a deep resonance to singing in the morning and praying in silence. *Buena lectura* (Good reading!) another pilgrim will say later, as I lace up my boots to hike to the next town. The nuns had asked me to read a special prayer for pilgrims in English out loud. One of the lines said: *do not be afraid.*

It felt like a sign. I think of myself high up on the *Los Ojos del Diablo* and know:

I am not.

—

My mind is wandering off to new places. Disoriented, I'm tottering along, looking left and right: I have no idea where I am these days. Except that I'm back and that things factually are the same yet everything feels different. As if someone woke up at night and moved all my furniture an inch to the side.

Someone (I) has moved all my furniture all the way back to an area I lived in, exactly one year ago. So the feeling is somewhat accurate. I'm physically back – five minutes away – to where I started. A reboot, a restart, a strange deja vu of some sort: who am I now? what was in-between? what is different?

The last day on the *Camino* looking over the soft hills of Güemes, the sunlight flooding the green meadows, piercing pearls of morning dew: resembling the flood inside of me, salty tears on my cheeks. The words of Ernesto the *Hospitalero* of my last *albergue* still ring in my ear, *this is really just the start. The Camino runs through you. You're always on it.*

It's hard to describe this feeling of living in a metaphor, visceral and tangible. For three weeks, life literally had been a path I was walking on. A stream of people all moving forward, towards a goal/the end, the importance of timing, new experiences waiting if you turned a corner, if you paused, went faster, slower, in circles and serpentines. People often describe life like this. But now I have lived it.

I have seen what happens if you skip a day and find yourself in a completely new group of pilgrims with new stories and various constellations. How you will never see some people again once you change your pace. How you sometimes do if you're lucky. Every opportunity is an invitation that you are always actively participating in, even when you're doing nothing. Even when you're taking a break. Every little thing is changing the course.

It's you and the *Camino*. It's you and life. Co-creating.

My mind is wandering off to new places. Disoriented, I'm tottering along, looking left and right: I have no idea where I am these days.

And I don't want to know. I don't need to know. This is new territory. This should not feel familiar. I should not be able to see where this path is going. As I am choosing it everyday anew. Letting it run through the person I am now.

I am changing and have changed and I don't know where that is leading but I know what a decision must feel like now.

Like a co-creation. A dance with life.

PARIS.

I could never live in Paris. I would say. Paris is my escape city. It is the place I escape to when everything else is falling apart. Where else would I go, if I was already living there?

The first time I went to Paris, I was in my late twenties doing a writer's residency in Zurich. A tiny room in the attic of a tall old-tenement building with a long winding wooden staircase leading up to a roof terrace that felt quite useless in mid-January. Later I would use the setting for the novel I still have not finished.

'Very romantic.' We repeated in different variations, trying to find new angles to look at the five square metres in front of us. "Do you smoke?" she asked eventually and I nodded, following her up the stairs to the roof terrace. Taking in the view or appearing to take in the view while thinking about her hairline, it was pretty high, giving her a ballerina's forehead. We smoked in silence. I had intentionally bought a pack of cigarettes at the train station for a moment like this, when you stand next to someone, gazing into the far far landscape. Thinking.

This is where it all begins.

Or something ordinary like that.

—

There's a small marble statue in the 11th arrondissement of Paris, of a woman standing on a pedestal, holding up the edges of her skirt filled with flowers, roses perhaps. *La Grisette de 1830* written on the plinth.

The first time I walked past her, looking at her posture, her chin high, proud and solitary, I stood still for a long time, observing. Something about her demeanour felt like looking into a mirror, a resonance, a twin. What was she doing here? Who was this woman, standing between two busy streets, almost unnoticed? Like an empress ruling the edge of Square Jules Ferry. No sign or explanation. Who put her here and why?

Good art speaks for itself, it reaches into you, however researching her story later enriches my initial feeling of familiarity. I find out that *La Grisette* is what they called young women in the late 17th century who were from a working-class background and "of lowly condition".[18] The name stems from the French word *gris* (grey) and refers to the cheap grey fabric of the dresses these women originally wore.

Later in the 19th century it would describe young women who were living independently without the supervision of their families, unmarried and mostly working "in the garment and millinery trade as seamstresses or shop assistants, the few occupations open to them in 19th century urban France, apart from domestic service."[19] Something that was quite unconventional at that time. There was also an allusion to sex work on the side and general promiscuity of these women, but that is so heavily coated in patriarchal views of that time, maybe they were just having boyfriends or lovers or they were receiving money for sex, maybe they were trying to break free from the conventional path of marriage and find love outside of it? Who knows.

When I think of *La Grisette*, I think of Mary Datchet, a character in Virginia Woolf's novel *Night and Day,* daughter of a vicar and technically not needing to work, she seeks her purpose in the support for the Suffragette movement, working for them in an office at Russell Square, feeling pure bliss "to get so much pleasure from simple things, such as eating one's breakfast alone in a room which had nice colours in it, clean from the skirting of the boards to the corners of the ceiling" and then going to work pretending to be "indistinguishable from the rest, and that when a wet day drove her to the Underground or omnibus, she gave and took her share of crowd and wet with clerks and typists and commercial men, and shared with them the serious business of winding-up the world to tick for another four-and-twenty hours."

Women enjoying their *delicious lives*, their furniture, their little trinkets, their rituals, their bodies, their clothes, their extensive minds, their sense of purpose of just being themselves.

Not everyone gets to carve their own path. For various reasons. Some are pushed into other obligations, not having the privilege to choose, or having to follow someone else's footsteps, some don't even realise it's an option, they've never even thought about it, just trotting along.

---

[18] *Dictionnaire de l'Académie française, Ed. from 1694*

[19] *Dictionnaire de l'Académie française, Ed. from 1694*

Some are pioneers without even realising it, they just can't help themselves.

More often than not, I find myself the latter, and the famous line from the Talking Heads song *Once in a lifetime* comes to mind:

–Well, how did I get here?

The Lost Empress

4

Don't be so high and mighty!

That's what you used to say.

—

The first man who told me to put my chin down was my boyfriend. It was about three or four weeks into the relationship, we were standing in the kitchen, cooking or doing the washing up. I was in my early twenties, telling him about something exciting, something I was proud of, I remember having a spark in my throat that I wanted to spit out. It was the second serious relationship I had ever been in and I guess I thought it was a normal thing to say.

Except that it wasn't and it annoyed me. But relationships are work right? We all need to compromise a little, so that the other person likes us a bit better. So that we fit right into the space, that they carve out for us, and if the head is a couple of inches too high it needs to be taken down a notch.

– Of course I am kidding. The problem is, he wasn't. He felt I was being arrogant with my chin so high and did I have to use so many English words when speaking German to him? *Was that really necessary?* He told me that I was only holding it high because my friend, the painter was doing it as well, that I had copied her body language and he did not appreciate it. It was a small incident, a little side-heap, that unfortunately later would turn into larger ones.

At this point I would like to state that I did not *put him completely in the bin* to paraphrase a favourite sentiment my painter friend likes to use for these situations but stayed in that relationship for a couple more years. A couple more pretty miserable years where I diluted my self-worth like pouring a bottle of champagne into the toilet. It was pretty much gone when I left him on a cold January morning, but I vowed something then and there. To never let that happen again. To never have a man or anyone truly undermine me in that way. To make sure that nobody was continuously hacking away on the very ground I was walking on.

In Deborah Levy's living memoir collection she talks about that problem in relationships, how she likes to see women swinging themselves on their high horses. Proud, full of self-worth, capable to manoeuvre. And that there's a certain tendency of men to drag those women down the minute they're up there.[20]

And then I met you. Exactly a decade later. *Don't be so high and mighty!* That's what you used to say. And I had forgotten. How it felt to be loved. Or undermined.

Or did I ever really know the difference?

–

There's a story that Heather Havrilesky writes about in one of her great Ask Polly columns about an ex who on the third date was telling

[20] see Deborah Levy, Real Estate

her how to pick up his dog's shit. How she felt weird about it. "It was a minor thing, but I remember getting this sick feeling like, what role am I auditioning for, here? If I'd paid attention to that feeling, I would've noticed that every step of the way, I was being primed to fit neatly into his life as a helpmate without needs or preferences."[21]

–

People don't like regret. But I regret people that I chose to be with. If I could go back and choose differently I would. *I can imagine better.* I don't think you have to have bad experiences. I don't understand why some people feel so reactive when I say that. "But you wouldn't be the person you are now. Experiences shape you." – I'm just being honest here. If I could *Eternal Sunshine of the Spotless Mind* all of this, I would. Because what I have learned (now, again,) is something that should have never been taken away from me in the first place.

I should have always felt loved and worthy.

It's interesting how breakups are never just about that particular heartbreak itself. One heartbreak is almost always a reflection of all the heartbreaks ever had, coming from somewhere deeper. And I guess that's where I am right now. At the core, the prehistoric wound. Where it all started.

–

There's a Tarot card, that symbolises a sudden dismantling like that: *The Tower*. People falling out of windows, lightning strikes, flames, the roof is falling off; *it's mayhem*. And it felt like *mayhem*. It was disorientating, devastating, disappointing but this card is also asking a question: who wants to live in a dark and gloomy tower on a rocky cliff anyway? *Haunted by ghosts?*

---

[21] https://www.askpolly.net/p/am-i-abusive: 26.01.2023

And I coming to terms with that. Leaving that tower behind me, to go out into the wilderness and look for horses. High horses, the highest I can find. Because I know how to ride them.

High and mighty.

fuck this then.

An Empress walks down Sonnenallee. A woman with long ashy hair. Her mouth is red and overflowing, blood dripping from its sides. In her hand, the heart of her lover.

Lilith said *fuck this then* and left Eden and Adam behind. If this is paradise, I want no part of it.

Anger is self-preserving.

She learned not to mask her rage with tears any longer.

People will break your heart, and not always in an obvious way: cheating and lying and leaving. Sometimes they will just be cold and neglectful and careless, occasionally rude and yelling, slightly demeaning. There's an itchy feeling but not enough to cut them off right away because there's hope, right? *They're not always like that.* There's always this story (some would call it an excuse) but it really is just an explanation and you're a good storyteller, and slowly they will trap you and you will participate gladly in the slow eroding of your sense of self. It will be a defeat of some sort, and until you realise it and you think you have to go all the way till the end because you cannot, under any circumstances, let *yourself* be defeated.

Sometimes it's hard to distinguish between being desperate and being hopeful. It is a very similar feeling.

There's a recurring idea that heartbreak is productive, that trauma can somehow be turned into art, that art needs pain to flourish. As a catalyst. And as someone who frequently wrote after intensely painful episodes in my life, to a bystander this might seem accurate.

And you'd think writing about my past relationships; the people I've dated would be upset that I write about them. And maybe they are. But you know, *me too*.

The irony of my life is that I dated three men in the last decade all different in age and nationality, however, interestingly similar scenarios played out, so if the shoe fits. These toxic relationship patterns are harrowing yet, unfortunately, not very *unique*.

And we all know this because most of us have heard, lived through both sides of most scenarios till a certain age. It's never new. It's always a series of unfortunate events that everyone but the protagonists could have predicted.

I'm afraid that I was never truly loved, all they did was try to love themselves. Desperately looking for validation, for someone to tell them how wonderful they are, how worthy, because they couldn't do that themselves. And maybe this is reciprocal, maybe I never truly loved them either.

Olivia Laing once said so poignantly: "All of my books start with somebody breaking up with me." I think the sentiment someone might conclude from this is a construed perspective to believe that pain is at the core of it. But it is not pain that sparks creativity but the final absence of it, the release of that burden you were carrying.

The reason I write after a heartbreak or dark times is because I am finally free to work again. Because the ghost that was causing me to be uninspired and unproductive has finally stopped rattling. I write because I am not having the heartbreak any longer. Writing creates that space. Art is my personal recognition of that.

I can only dream of the artist I would be if all of *this* didn't happen to me. I have always enjoyed writing. I was inventing stories as a child because I liked it, because it was fun to dream. And then because I had to.

—

There is this fear of being happy, which is not apparent for everyone to see, but it is happiness most people fear I think. It's the responsibility of a good life, the feeling of a more painful fall, no one can take it away if you've never had it. But I think it is not just happiness I am afraid of. I am afraid of being powerful. I am afraid of taking up too much space, of being too much.

Yet I yearn for it. As a child I dreamed of being a witch, the most powerful being, one who can will things into existence, everything she desires is at her whim. There's a reason children think they have magical powers, because *who wouldn't want them?*

But when you're constantly told a different story, that somehow there is no space for you, that you are not allowed to shut the door, that you don't have sovereignty over your own body—

There's a part of me that is still haunted by the ghosts who didn't want to write about all of this. Who wanted to lie in bed hiding under the covers, shutting my eyes tightly and let time pass by, *let time deal with it*. But time doesn't change anything, it is pure human will that does.

—

Fuck this then, Lilith said. She knew that the world created for her, the one she was born into, made for, wasn't accepting of how she was. Being Adam's first wife, made from the same clay, by God, his equal. If *he* couldn't handle it, she had her own things to do. Her own things to fight for. New ground. A world of her own. Far away from paradise. Even if that meant being written out of the story, erased, turned into *a lacuna*.

A lost Empress, unnoticed.

There seems to be little to do for enlightened women in folklore and literature but either to leave and become murderous demons or simply to die.

Like Malina in Ingeborg Bachmann's novel of the same name, disappearing through a crack in the wall or Empress Elisabeth of Austria jumping ship at the end of the film *Corsage*. Like *Thelma & Louise* riding off the cliff, into the abyss, escaping the grasps of the police but dead nonetheless.

There were times in my teens and twenties where I was certain I wouldn't make it beyond my thirties because of this narrative that women that are odd, or weird, or simply just speaking their minds, that there is an underlying threat of insanity and subsequent suicide, or that the only freedom to exist for these women is beyond this world, so they choose death, and I am so tired of it.

I remember my mother telling me when I was a young girl how a close friend of hers became mentally ill, just that she didn't say it that way. I could hear her fear, creeping out, *another ghost.* One must be careful. Must be *normal.*

Or how I would read plays by Sarah Kane at Uni and afterwards discuss with a friend how we both were terrified of a similar fate.

I remember my old therapist in Berlin saying that at her age now she doesn't feel at risk.

And I just think: fuck this.

A certain death is required after all. But it's not mine. And like *Lady Lazarus* who came back from the dead, we need to learn how to resurrect. Again and again.

Filling the *lacunae*, the words are overflowing in my mouth.

Acknowledgements

Thank you.

To my parents. Always.

To my wonderful editor Terri-Jane Dow.

To the Edinburgh Central Library where most of this book was written, a refuge for a writer on low income to work in peace, to look up every once in a while and marvel at the beautiful domed ceiling.

A very BIG THANK YOU to the mega supporters:

Janina Rook
Monica Dear
Michael Grandjean
Linda Hembeck
Maren Zurek

And to all the other generous and supportive people who made a pledge on the Kickstarter and Paypal campaign that made the first printing of this book possible.

I couldn't have done it without you.

Sophia Hembeck is a writer and visual artist based in Edinburgh. Originally from Germany, she is writing in English and German. She has studied playwriting at the University of Arts in Berlin.

Books

Things I Have Noticed – Essays on leaving/searching/finding (2020)
Januar (2018)
This Feeling of Emptiness – Like Shopping For Groceries And Forgetting To Bring The Pfandflaschen (2017)

Find the latest at

www.museletterpublishing.com
www.themuseletter.substack.com

Instagram: @sophiahembeck

"I'd like the one without the existential dread, please."

"Most writers produce their memoirs a lot later in life. After they have written their fiction, their stories, they sail into their own life to examine. So in many ways I'm doing this backwards. It's not intentional. It just sort of happened. Like a hole in a pipe it just started leaking. At first a soft dribble that would find its way into my fiction. Thinking I had it under control, not realising after a while that the bucket I had put under it was overflowing and flooding everything overnight. This is all that was washed ashore. Those days. These are the things I have noticed."

The first book of the poetic memoir series written by Sophia Hembeck.

www.museletterpublishing.com